I0429139

The Frugal Prepper
Survival on a Budget

By Robert Paine

© 2014

Prepare for Survival Without Breaking the Bank!

We all need to prep. Nobody knows what the future will bring. But, prepping doesn't need to cost you your life savings! You don't need to spend money on every latest gadget and toy, every item marketed as a "must-have" or a "life-saver".

The Frugal Prepper: Survival on a Budget will guide you and your family through the important steps and considerations that you need to begin prepping without spending a lot of money.

In this book you will learn how to:
- Which foods and supplies you need to store for survival, and how to find them for the lowest price possible.
- Pack a Bug Out Bag for each member of your family, without going overboard.
- Fortify your home and yourself for ultimate safety and protection.
- Clever ways to cut costs and save big while prepping.
-And much, much more!

Sign up for Robert's Mailing List to be notified of **New Releases**

and **Special Sales**: http://eepurl.com/zvm11

Prepping is a hobby for some, a lifestyle for many, and a way to make sure that our families are protected should anything happen. "So, what exactly *could* happen?" many people ask. Well, in reality, anything could happen - preppers come from all walks of life and are preparing for vastly different things. Some are simply concerned that a natural disaster might strike where they live and they would not be prepared. Take Hurricane Katrina or the Moore, Oklahoma tornado, for example. Those instances reinforce the fact that natural disasters do happen and, for those that were prepared, they were able to access food and water while FEMA and other rescuers worked on restoring power. For those that were unprepared, well, we saw the worst possible outcomes. You don't want to be one of the ones left behind.

For other people, they are prepping for the end. The Big End. You know who you are. These preppers are serious about doing everything possible to prepare for the worst-case scenario. They may live off the grid, or at least know *how* to, should the need arise, and they teach their entire families to live that way as well. They are the ones that live in more rural areas, where land is cheaper and survival skills are necessary just for their day-to-day lives. Natural disasters happen, doomsday can easily happen and perhaps an economic apocalypse could happen as well. There are many different scenarios that could require us to have prepping and survival skills, so it makes sense to start gathering those skills now, no matter which scenario we think is the most likely.

Today there are millions of individuals and families working feverishly to get prepared for their worst fears or for those events that we all know are coming, sooner or later. They are working hard, and doing very well at it. Prepping is something that, for many people, has become a secret lifestyle. But, regardless of how or why you prep, one of the most common misconceptions about prepping is that it takes a lot of money. Sure, you could spend hundreds of thousands of dollars buying every fancy toy and gadget that claims it will save you and your loved ones. Most of that is just marketing lies. But prepping doesn't have to be that way. Some people become extreme preppers, able to live on very little every month, while others are just accustomed to living frugally. There is a family in Pasadena, California living off 6,000 pounds of produce a year, which all comes from their property. They grow more food than they need and sell the excess to restaurants. Of course, we can't all do that in our situations, but there are always concrete steps that we can take to prep smarter and more cheaply to save money for other purposes.

What is Prepping?

Prepping is simply the action or process of preparing something for use later or preparing *for* something (an event) that may come in the future. Sure, there are those preppers that live on the fringe of society with their thirty-year food pantries, bunkers, and arsenal of mines, bombs, booby traps, grenades, guns, rifles and the like. That's great, if your lifestyle supports that. But for the rest of us, prepping takes time and time is money. What if you need to prep on a budget?

Running to the store last minute to stock up is not an option if you have to collect your family or fortify your home when disaster strikes. Never mind the fact that the rest of city has the same idea. You would be lucky to even make it to the store. The roads would be cluttered, backed up with stop and go traffic. Or worse, they would be blocked off or not usable at all. And even if you make it to the store, the shelves would be cleaned out at best and, at worse, rioting would have already broken out so you wouldn't be able to get the things you need anyways. No, you need a better plan.

Prepping is the best way to give you and your family a good chance to survive any catastrophe. First, you need to know what you are preparing for or against. There are five main factors that lead to death in a survival situation. These are dehydration, starvation, weather, natural situations, and sanitation. To combat these, you'll want to create an emergency pantry composed of water, food, clothes (shoes and blankets too), security (home defense and personal defense), as healthy and clean a living environment as can be provided, and knowledge of various situations and how to best handle those situations. 'Situations' is an all-inclusive term, but could be anything from a spider bite to an angry mob at your front door. 'Situations' can also include mold, illnesses, infections, and depletion of your emergency pantry due to negligence, theft or disaster.

I know what you're thinking: "There are way too many things to possibly be able to plan for!" It can seem overwhelming, certainly, but that's just the start of things. Planning what you want to stock and how you plan to store it is only a third of the battle. Another third of the battle is acquiring knowledge, the proper mindset, and the right skills to succeed in your endeavors. The rest is actually getting the supplies that you need and checking them off of your list to ensure you have everything you need.

Before you start buying up everything in sight, or decide your goal is unobtainable and simply give up, do not get discouraged by the work that lies ahead. Start gradually and aim small. Make a list of the most basic things that you think your family will need to survive. Do some research on this. High profile freeze-dried foods store well and are tasty but they are also very expensive for the average family. And there is no need to buy food that you and your family normally do not consume. The same thing goes for every other category of supply you'll need. But you have to start somewhere, so start with a list of everything you think you'll need. Be as broad as possible, because it's far easier to take things off of the list later, then to try and remember things you have forgotten to add to the list in the first place.

Prepping on a budget is certainly a different way of preparing, because until anything happens at all, the bills keep coming and life goes on. Building a bunker or camping in the wilderness does not provide a steady income like your job does, unfortunately. Finding the time to dedicate to prepping is a challenge because time is money. However, prepping is not just a hobby to do in leisure time. It is a lifestyle, and one that you and your family can adopt without breaking the bank.

Another challenge to prepping on a budget is diligence. Not sticking to your budget with the intent to make it up next week is an example of a common slip up. When you slack in your preparations, it gets easier *to continue to* slack in your preparations. No one is going to sit you down with an intervention when nothing has even happened yet. Rest assured that pointing fingers and the blame game creates enough stress to have you hesitating and second-guessing yourself. Hesitation in a hostile situation could be fatal. Prepping keeps your body, mind, and spirit sharp and fit. For when disaster strikes, it will be too late to "get into shape".

Prepping on a budget takes time and your efforts may seem trivial when you focus on the small, day-to-day items. Yes, it may seem like you are counting pennies, cutting coupons in your free time, and your emergency pantry doesn't look like much. It is easy to give up the plan when nothing appears to have happened. But the little things add up. Before you know it, you'll have more supplies than you realized. And if anything does happen, you and your family will be better fit to survive than if you had done nothing at all.

Prepping on a budget gives you time for trial and error. Learning what foods store well and which ones don't is a part of the process and figuring it out after a disaster usually does not bode well. Prepping on a budget hones your negotiation skills, if you go to flea markets or garage sales for some of your supplies. Other benefits include sharpening your mind and strengthening your resolve. If you have emergency food supplies for 6 months but have no concept of rationing, healthy vs. meager portions, or the self-discipline to stick to the meal rations, then your level of preparedness is not going to be that great. Sticking to a budget will train you to focus on the things that are most important, and this knowledge and way of thinking will seep over into other parts of your life as well, creating even more benefits.

Prepping on a budget usually leads to better budgeting choices in general. You and your family will benefit from prepping on a budget. And it can be a fun experience for a family to do together that doubles as a lifeline. The gradual change is best when including your family and is a preferred method to the culture shock of simply telling or demanding that your family do things a certain way one day, with no reasoning in the build up. Now that you know some challenges and benefits to prepping on a budget, let's look at what you should actually start to prep.

In order to become more independent and build up a self-sustaining prepping habit, there are a few "big picture" things you can start to think of and begin to do to get started, including:

- Become less dependent on your job
- Get out of debt
- Reduce monthly expenses
- Buy some land
- Learn to grow your own food
- Find a reliable source of water nearby or learn how to sterilize water

- Explore alternative energy sources

When you are about to begin your prepping lifestyle, it's important to remember that you should never have to go into debt just because you are prepping. Prepping is about being responsible and that includes paying close attention to your finances. Now is not the time to go into a bunch of debt, simply because you want to have every latest gadget and survival toy. The basics of prepping can be started with little or no money, and these money-saving principles will come back to help you all along your survival way.

To begin your prepping journey, you should always ask yourself: what you are doing this for? What scenarios can you envision happening? And if those happen, what will you need? What is the minimum amount of money or goods that you and your family can survive on? Your family needs to be able to survive, of course, but you don't need to be in debt to prepare for it. Prepping for an unknown future economic reality or otherwise is important. So important that everyone should be able to do it, regardless of their current financial situation.

Once you begin to understand what it is you need to have on hand, it can then become something that you work on to keep you focused and, of course, up to date with your prepping needs. What do you need to have on hand to begin with? It's easy to start. First, understand that you can pick up a few things to begin with as you start your journey to prepperhood. As the months go by, you will begin to notice that your collection will grow, continuously. The more you pick up and store, the longer you'll be able to survive, of course. But it will be fulfilling to see your survival collection grow over the months as you pick up various items when and where it makes most sense to do so.

Prioritizing different areas of your life to become a prepper or survivalist can be wildly successful *if* you stick to a budget and work from it. Chances are, if you have watched any prepping shows, or read any survival blogs, you have seen the massive amounts of items that some people have in their storage areas in case of an emergency. You don't necessarily need to compare yourself to these people. You are not going to need every single thing that they have and the sooner you start tailoring your prepping habits to your family and your specific needs and goals, the easier it will become. You and your family are unique. You have different needs, desires, and abilities than every other family out there. Shouldn't your prepping lifestyle reflect that?

Consider your budget and your family's necessary needs and cut back on items that you obviously don't need. Do you need to dine out every week? Certainly not, and that $30-40 or more could go to your prepping budget. Cable, movies, and other forms of entertainment can be cut back and cut down to allow for more money in your prepping arsenal. You can at least scrounge between $300-400 a month extra for prepping in this manner. Then, after your have worked on your budget and have started to save money, you can start actually buying what you need!

What to Prep

In the interest of gradually transitioning to a prepper lifestyle, it's best to start out with an Every Day Carry (EDC). An EDC refers to those items that you carry on you throughout the day. Of course you will have your phone, car keys, and wallet, but, in terms of prepping, decide which other items would benefit you in any situation. In addition to what you already carry, here is a good place to start:

- Pocket Knife, Multitool, or Swiss Army Knife
- Para-cord Survival Bracelet
- A lighter (Windproof is better)
- Watch

These items are lightweight and can even be carried in a cigarette case or aluminum wallet for consolidation. The idea is to help you help yourself. It's not a rescue mission, but these items can help you get yourself into a better position for a rescue mission. Another important point to note is that these items should stay on your person at all times. They do not stay in your car, on your desk, in the jacket pocket of the coat you just hung up, or in your purse. If you're going to be able to use them, they need to be with you, so get in the habit of keeping your EDC on you at all times.

The next step in prepping that you will want to consider is creating a Bug Out Bag (BOB). A BOB is designed to aid you in getting out of the way of danger as quickly and efficiently as possible. If a tornado touches down nearby while you're driving, outrunning it may not be an option. You may have to leave the car and head for safety. You may be close to home or you may be nowhere near your home. But, with a bug out bag, you will have food, water, and other items to aid you in toughing out the storm, or any other survival situation you may find yourself in. So, what goes in your Bug Out Bag, exactly? Well, first off, you will want to start with a large backpack to put it all in. One that fits well, is comfy and easy to carry, but with enough storage to fit all the items you want to carry. Here are some items for you and your family to include:

Nutrition:
- Meal Replacement Bars for 24 hours to 72 hours. That's 3-10 bars per person, roughly.
- Bottle of Water for each meal (3-10 bottles, per person)

Supplies:
- Pocketknife, Combat Knife or Multitool
- Waterproof Matches, Lighter, and maybe Cottons Ball soaked in Petroleum Jelly (highly flammable)
- First Aid Kit, Sewing Kit, Flashlight, Batteries
- Toilet Paper, Sunscreen, Bug Spray
- Spare personal medicine or prescription glasses (if you wear glasses)

Defense:

- Stun Gun, Baton, Pepper Spray

General:
- Spare Change of Clothes Including socks and underwear
- Toothbrush/Baking Soda
- Tarp, Para-cord Bracelet, Sleeping Bag, Blankets, Handwarmers

These items will meet your basic needs for one to three days (depending on how many days you prepare for). They will also aid in giving you more time to find help or get yourself in a better position as far as nutrition, shelter and situations go. Keep bug out bags for all members of your family, as creating one is a great way to get your kids involved and invested in their future as well.

Bug Out Bags can also be kept in your home in addition to in your vehicle. Even if you fortify your home, you may still find yourself in a compromising position where leaving your home is a wiser decision than staying. Repeat the BOB process and create one for your vehicle as well as your home. That way, no matter if you stay or go, you'll have access to your BOB and a few extra days of survival. Again, ensure that each member in your party has a bug out bag prepared.

Ways to Cut Costs

Food and water is a huge part of survival, obviously. Without it, we don't even stand a chance. Acquiring what you need can be broken down into three questions: 1) How many months do you want your emergency pantry to last? 2) What is the minimum amount that you and your family need? 3) How much is your family's budget?

The important thing to remember about prepping on a budget is to simply take the next step. Don't get caught up in the huge end picture all of the time. Focus on what you can do today, you're your first step will be, and work to achieve that. Even if you start out with buying just one extra can of food a week, it is one extra can in your emergency pantry. If that is all that you can manage for the next year, by the end of that year, you will have 52 cans in your emergency pantry. Not bad at all.

One way to save money while building your emergency pantry is to cut coupons for the items that are on your list. This is something that your family can participate in. Another way to save money is to become a rewards customer. Many major and minor grocery stores have a rewards cards or clubs that reward shoppers with gift cards, savings in fuel, or special club discounts. You can couple your club discounts with your coupons and get near double the savings. Do some research on which stores carry the products that you need and find coupons for those items. Some grocery stores even have online coupons that you can access in the store or you can have them emailed to you. Thrift stores are another way to build up your emergency pantry. Many thrift stores have 1/2 off sales pretty regularly. That's the time to shop. Again, remember your list and your budget and stick to it. Visit different thrift stores for what you need.

Buying supplies in bulk can create huge savings. If you purchase a case of canned goods and that total equals your prepping budget for the month, you might think it's a bad idea at first. But, remember, you won't need to purchase any more canned goods after that month, and can focus on other items from your list. Use your time and money wisely. Research the other items on your list and get your coupons ready. See what's on sale this week or this month and focusing on knocking those items off of your list.

Networking with other people in your mindset can provide information and tips to help you and your family in your task.

Last but not least, learn to fix, patch, reuse and re-task. Patching up clothes and fixing tools or equipment is an invaluable skill that will more than come in handy should you have to delve into your survival pantry. And, when you cannot fix or patch an item, re-task it. Just about anything can be multipurpose. It's a good idea to do some research and get hands-on experience with building and repairing. You can even visit some workshops or free seminars on this subject. You don't have to be an expert in everything and anything, but it helps to have some idea of where to begin.

Building a Survival Food Pantry on a Budget

Prices of everything are going up, and our earnings are drastically down across most every industry. For some of us, this means that we are living on the edge of poverty, striving to pay our bills and get through each week, living paycheck to paycheck. Food and supplies are the first thing we need to survive. The shelves in any store are stocked, but in an instant, when a natural disaster or another emergency strikes, those shelves will be emptied. Losing your job, having a personal crisis, or a national tragedy can affect your ability to feed your family and yourself. Grocery stores have stocks of food right now, but that can change as well. They used to have larger warehouse areas that had the ability to keep restocking, but most stores these days are limited to a 3-day supply of goods. That's including the stock that they have in the back. If anything happened to the trucks or the ships coming with food, then the grocery stores will run out. That's if there is not already a huge surge in people buying before a crisis, which we have seen in past disasters is almost always the case.

What would happen today if you could not leave your home? Would you have enough food to last a week? What about a month? If the answer is yes, then congratulations - you are doing a great prepping job. You are also one of the few prepared ones. But, if the answer is no, then you are not living off-grid or prepping at all. You need to do this, for you and your family, and you need to make sure that you have the food in the pantry starting this week. If you have extra food, it should be enough for at least two weeks minimum, but you don't need to go overboard and stock a year's worth of food right away. This will ensure you will not have to choose between buying food and paying a mortgage.

Decide first - how much money can you spend? And if you do not have a budget for food prepping, then start looking at where your money goes. Stretch your earnings, and look at what you are spending your money on. For instance, do you really, really need that $4.00 cup of joe from the local high-priced coffee shop? No, I think not. Do you need the junk food? No, you don't. Can you cook from scratch and save money? Yes, though it may not save time, it will most certainly save you money in the long run.

When building your pantry, you will want enough food for you and your family to eat everyday for at least 6 to 12 months. There are emergency pantry calculators online that help you calculate your family's minimum food storage needs. For a family of 4, a 6-month emergency pantry is usually suggested as follows:

600 lbs. of Grain – This includes rice, oats, corn meal, wheat, and flour.

26 lbs. of Fats – These come in the form of cooking oils, shortening, and peanut butter

120 lbs. of Beans & Peas – This includes Pinto, Lima, and Soy beans. It also includes, peas, dry soup mix, and legumes.

300 lbs. of Cooking Essentials – Essentials means honey, sugar, jams, dehydrated milk, evaporated milk, baking soda, baking powder, salt, vinegar, and water.

The emergency pantry calculator can be a starting point for your pantry and help guide you and your family towards storing enough food for 6 months. When beginning an emergency pantry, keep in mind that the numbers used to calculate the pounds of food for storage are based on the average minimum amount of 1200-

calorie consumption daily. It's not a hard rule but there are side effects to meager meals. Starvation leaves the person sluggish with little energy. The muscles begin to atrophy without protein to keep them strong. Fatigue and weight loss of lean muscle are major effects of not eating enough and are detrimental to survival of any situation. The goal is to stay as healthy as possible while rationing your pantry, so you may want to up those baseline amounts if you plan on eating over 1200 calories per person, per day.

When building an emergency pantry, remember to also store water. Easy to forget, but a deadly mistake if you do. Most food expands in the stomach when coupled with water. This helps to digest the food and gives a feeling of fullness. The foods that you prepare may also require water, of course, yet this is one area that preppers often overlook. You can purchase 5 gallon jugs, 1 liter bottles, cases of water or create your own water storage system, just so long as you have what your and your family needs. You will need it to cook, to drink, to wash your clothes, and to wash yourself. Keep this in mind as your begin your emergency food pantry.

The foods that you want to stockpile the most are the ones that are protein rich and provide the most nutritional bang for their buck. Unopened boxes or bags of cereal are safe to consume for up to 8 months and make for a quick light breakfast. Foods high in energy and protein such as peanut butter, nuts and granola bars are a great addition to any emergency pantry. Dehydrated fruits are also protein rich and last anywhere from 6 months to 1 year. Below are a few ideas of the main types of foods you will want to start stocking:

Canned Soups – Ready-to-eat soups can often be eaten without heating. Pour some water in and you're ready to go. Sure, we're used to them hot, but the same nutrients are there, regardless of the temperature. There are many varieties such as vegetable, beef, chicken, tomato and more. Many ready-to-eat canned soups are also manufactured with an easy quick-pop lid that doesn't require a can opener. This includes canned chili. Look for those and you'll be good.

Canned fruits and vegetables – Stock up on canned pasta sauce, green beans, peas, carrots, corn, grapefruit, oranges, and any other of your preferred fruits and vegetables. These canned vegetables have a shelf life of up to 3 years and still remain nutritious with protein, vitamins, and antioxidants.

Canned meats – These include tuna, chicken, spam, and salmon. Meat will be in short supply either because the grocery markets have been ransacked or because there's no longer any meat production. Meat is a source of iron and protein. Buy in bulk and buy on sale. Typically have a very long shelf life so you can feel safe buying in bulk to store.

Pasta – Pasta has little water content and stores for up to 2 years in a cool, dark space in an airtight container. Pasta provides for a quick meal. You can improvise by adding canned meat and vegetables to get a nutritious and filling dinner. Avoid stockpiling pastas with egg because this type of pasta has a small amount of fat in it that can break down over time and begin to smell and spoil.

Dehydrated Potatoes – These have a shelf life of a couple years. Be aware of the fact that some instant mashed potatoes mixes add butter and dry milk for flavor, resulting in a reduced shelf life.

Packaged meals – Ramen noodles, macaroni and cheese, and dinner pasta mixes are a good way to mix up the meals so that you and your family aren't eating the same drab meal night after night. Add variety with your canned meats and vegetables.

One thing you don't want to forget in your emergency pantry is cooking spices and ingredients such as vinegar, baking powder, or baking soda. You can even include chicken, beef, and vegetable bouillon cubes. They don't take up a lot of room and help create soups and stews. For your cooking oils, you will want to store vegetable-based oils. These are oils such as olive oil, coconut oil, and vegetable oil. They won't spoil for years, unlike some animal-based oils. An emergency pantry isn't about eating excruciatingly obnoxious survival food, astronaut food, or any other kind of food, except for what you and your family normally eat. When you are deciding which food to buy in bulk, consider its shelf life as well. The following foods store the longest and are a cost-efficient addition to any emergency pantry:

Corn Meal – 12-month shelf life.

Peppercorns – 1-3 years shelf life.

Powdered Milk – 2 years normally, but if kept at a cool 40 degrees Fahrenheit will last up to 10 years.

Regular Sugar-Free 1 Minute or 5 Minute Oatmeal – 2-3

years

Dried Split Peas – 4-5 years (will last indefinitely with O2 Absorbers in an airtight container – more on those below)

Vitamins – 4-5 years shelf life.

1200 to 3600 Calorie Food Bars - 5 years

These food bars are relatively inexpensive calorie ration food bars that are packed with nutrition and are great for your pantry or Bug Out Bags. The trick to getting the savings is to buy in bulk. A 72-hour supply is usually ten dollars at the most. But a 20-day supply is sold for up to 33% off in savings.

Rolled Oats – Up to 28 years when stored oxygen free. Portion your oats into airtight plastic containers with oxygen absorbers to allow for maximum shelf life, easier usage, and rotation.

White Rice – 4-5 years. Oxygen free white rice will last 25-30 years. Again, portion your rice into airtight plastic containers with oxygen absorbers to allow for maximum shelf life, easier usage, and rotation.

Dried Pinto Beans and Lentils– Indefinite. They are a great source of high protein, vitamins, and fiber while being low maintenance, low fat and low cost.

Honey – Indefinite. Honey also has medicinal application because of its antibacterial activity.

Sugar – Indefinite

Salt – Indefinite

While they aren't necessary for your pantry, oxygen absorbers are most definitely prudent and can significantly extend the shelf life of your stored foods. Oxygen absorbers can mean a difference of decades in terms of shelf life. Oxygen can cause mold, spoilage, nutritional oxidation, condensation, and attract bugs. It's not enough to quickly store food; even in an already airtight container, oxygen is already in there. The solution is to invest in oxygen absorbers.

Oxygen absorbers are little pouches of iron oxide. They aren't edible but they are safe to use around your food, don't leak toxins, and don't alter your food in any way. The oxygen absorbers are measured in "CC" or "cubic centimeters". So, a 2000cc oxygen absorber will absorb 2000 cubic centimeters of oxygen. The general rule is to use 2000cc of oxygen absorbers per 5-gallon bucket. Oxygen makes up about 21% of air and the right amount of oxygen absorbers can take that percentage down to .01%.

Some preppers will even store rice and beans in 2 liter beverage bottles. They are food safe and colored plastics can help protect against light exposure, which also break down stored foods. Just add an oxygen absorber or two and tighten the lid.

5-gallon food grade buckets can be purchased in sets of 3-5 buckets for $20 to $25 online. You can get 10 Mylar Bags for 5-gallon buckets and a quantity of 10 Oxygen Absorbers at 2000cc a piece for $20 to $30 online. Just be sure to check the bags for leaks before filling them. A good way to do this is to shine a flashlight in the bags, in a dark room.

Oxygen absorbers are packaged in an airtight plastic. Once broken, the absorbers will start to absorb. So, it is practical to have your buckets or 2-liters or storage container already filled with food before opening the oxygen absorbers. Never leave oxygen absorbers out for more than 30 minutes or they will expire. Insert them into the food and close the container airtight. The remaining absorbers can be kept in another airtight container, such as a Mason jar. Fill it up with rice to reduce the amount of oxygen in the jar.

Back to acquiring your emergency pantry foods: gardening can be a fun, family affair and it's a good way to get your family involved in preparedness. Growing your own food is a useful skill that puts you and your family one step closer to your goal and far ahead of the average family these days. One thing to consider when gardening is to only grow foods that your family actually eats. Another thing to consider is that you want to grow foods that produce more than one vegetable or fruit per plant or produces more than one harvest.

Here are a few vegetables that are easy to grow and some tips to help you along the way:

Carrots are easy to plant. They grow underground and don't require a bunch of fuss. You can even grow them in pots; just make sure the pot is deep enough. When the carrot tops come through the soil, they are ready to harvest.

Lettuce and Spinach have many different varieties to choose

from and are easy to maintain. Lettuce is partial to cooler weather so planting in the spring or fall is adequate. Sow new seeds every 2 to 3 weeks to spread out your harvest.

Tomato plants only need a bit of water and lots of sun. They will grow all summer long and continue to produce fruit as well.

Sweet potatoes are very resilient. They can be grown in imperfect soil and hot weather. Wait about one month after the last freeze to give the ground time to warm up.

Bush beans are another great and easy to plant vegetable for your garden. Some well-drained soil and a lot of sun make for the perfect bed for sowing. Once again, continue to sow seeds every 2-3 weeks to keep a continuous harvest going.

Seeds are inexpensive to buy and these easy-to-grow foods don't require hours of care or any special type of fertilizer. When considering storage options, vegetables and meats can be canned at home using a pressure canner. Pressure canning is method used to preserve food low in acid. This includes meats, poultry, fish, chili, and vegetables. It's similar to regular canning with the added element of pressure that depends on your altitude. The pressure is very important to processing low-acidic or alkaline foods at a higher temperature. The bacteria botulism dies at the boiling water temperature, but its spores may survive. So, the extra added pressure heats the water to a higher temperature. It is for this reason, when canning vegetables, meats, and fish, that a pressure canner, which is different from a pressure cooker, is used and used right.

Pressure cookers cost $100 and upwards and may be out of your budget range now and in the foreseeable future. Another option for your vegetable harvests is that you and your family can sell leftover produce from your garden and put the money saved towards your emergency pantry.

Canning with fruits and tomatoes or tomatoes sauce (which is actually a fruit) may be a more cost effective canning option for your budget. Ball Regular-Mouth Mason jars with lids and bands can be purchased in cases of 12 anywhere from $10 and upwards. The canned goods can be stored safely in your pantry for at least 1 year, so long as they are used before 2 years.

Waterbath canning is a time-tested process that has been used for ages. This method can be used to can fruits, jams, jellies, applesauce, salsa, and tomatoes. This process requires a large stockpot, at least 7 1/2 inches in height and 9 1/2 wide. Fill it with enough water to cover the mason jars by an inch and boil. Wash your mason jars, lids and bands. Warming up the jars in hot dishwater eliminates the chance of breakage when they are filled with hot foods.

The recipes used for preparing your fruits, jams, jellies or pickles range from varieties that include Pectin (a gelling agent) to those that don't include Pectin or any other agents. As long as the concoction remains acidic, you can use the waterbath process while being creative. Once your food is prepared, add it to the Mason jars, leaving about an inch of headspace. Stir and smash the food to each side of the Mason jar to remove bubbles. After you wipe the rims of the jars, center the lid on the top of the Mason jar and apply the band until it is fingertip tight. This allows ample room for air bubbles to escape during the waterbath. Insert the filled and topped mason jars into the stockpot and keep the water at least an inch above the Mason jar. Put the stockpot lid back on the pot. Your recipe will have an amount of time to let the jars boil. Remember to take into account your altitude. Basically, add 5 minutes for every 3,000 feet that you are above sea level.

After boiling the jars for the appropriate amount of time, remove from heat and let the jars stand 5 minutes. Then remove the jars, keeping them upright, and place them on a rack or kitchen towel and counter to cool. You want the jars to cool for 8 to 12 hours to complete the process and complete the seal. After 8 to 12 hours, test the seal by pushing it with your finger. If it rebounds, then the jar isn't sealed properly. Another way to test the seal is to tap the bottom of the jar with a teaspoon. If the sound is dull, the jar may not be sealed properly. What you're listening for is a high-pitched ring. The last way to test the seal is to view the seal at eye level. If it isn't concave (caved it), but it is flat or bulging, then the jar may not be sealed properly. If an improper seal is the case, the canned goods can still be refrigerated and used by you and your family, but should not be stored for extended periods of time.

You may experience variations in color or consistency in your home canned products. That doesn't mean that the products are dangerous for consumption. Know what normal home canning variations look like. A brown color or darker color is typically caused by oxidation or a breakdown in the color of the food, as in the case of apples or guacamole. Soft texture in food is caused by a breakdown in food or plant tissue due to heat. Crystals in canned fish is a result of pressure canning Magnesium Ammonium Phosphate, which is in fish. Crystals in fruits are caused by a high acidic salt compound but they are still safe to consume. Metal cans (some people still home-can goods with actual cans) may leave bits of metal or a metallic taste on the food. And, when the food is above the juice line in the jar, it is still safe for consumptions as long as the seal remains intact.

Signs of bad jars or cans are if it's badly dented, leaking or rusting. If the jar or can has a broken seal or it spurts upon opening, then the food inside has been compromised. As a general rule of common sense, always inspect the jar or can with your eyes and nose. If there is a strange odor or appearance, then discard it – it's not worth the risk to the health of you and your family.

When building your emergency pantry, you will also want to consider vitamin-infused powder, purchased in bulk when possible. Seeds are another item that you may want to keep in supply. It would be handy should your emergency pantry deplete before your situation resolves.

Trade and bartering may come in handy in a world where supermarkets no longer exist. Letting your family try their bartering skills at a flea market is one way to get them involved in preparedness. Another way to get your family involved is to have them cut coupons for fruits (to can) when they are on sale and getting them involved in a relatively inexpensive ($30 or less) canning process. When storing your successfully canned goods, remember to label them with the date made, the ingredients, and the expiration date.

How the food is stored is an important part of maintaining your emergency pantry. You will want an easy-to-understand inventory system that allows for easy rotation of foods. You can achieve this. Label all cans, jars, buckets, and bags with the date acquired or date manufactured, and the expiration date, and ingredients. You want your emergency pantry to remain at cool consistent temperature and a dark, dry space. Teach your family the labeling system so that everyone can easily know how to read the labels and determine what is safe to eat.

Water

As mentioned before, five common factors of death in a survival situation are dehydration, starvation, weather, situations, and sanitation. Dehydration is when the body needs water and doesn't have it. It is one of the quickest forms of death in a survival situation, and one of the most easily avoidable. Some symptoms are:
- Increased thirst, dry mouth, and swollen tongue
- Inability to sweat, decreased or concentrated urine output
- Weakness, dizziness, fatigue and fainting
- Diarrhea, fever, headaches, and seizures

When storing emergency water, allot each person in your

plan one gallon per day. So for a family of 4, you would need four gallons of water for each day you plan for. For 6 months, that amounts to 745 gallons of water. And, that's just for consumption, not even taking into account the water you need for cooking, bathing, and cleaning.

How does one go about collecting 750 gallons of water? One idea is to collect rainwater. Rainwater collection has been around for centuries. It is used even by states that are known to have deserts and those that experience severe droughts. One square foot of rain on the average roof in certain climates can amount to 600 gallons of water per year, if collected properly. If you have gutters, you can divert the water already collected on your roof into your water storage barrels via your gutters. Invest in a gutter filter to prevent leaves, sticks, and other debris from clogging up your system. You will want 2-4 food grade water barrels connected via hose adapters and a hose. The extra water barrels serve as an overflow system once the first barrel is full. Some people even add an extra hose to the last barrel in the chain and position the hose downhill and away from their home. This ensures that any extra overflow diverts downhill and doesn't collect in the basement of their home.

When collecting rainwater, understand that it may still need filtering and purification before being fit to drink. Another thing to consider when collecting rainwater is that you may need a permit in some counties and states, or it may be illegal altogether (crazy, I know!). Do your research and know your facts and the law to avoid being caught up in the system. That's valuable time that you could be investing towards you and your family's survival plan.

The barrels used for water storage should be food grade. Yes, this was already mentioned, but it is vitally important, so I'm mentioning it again. The barrels specifically manufactured for water storage come with a spout, leaf filter, and overflow value and can be purchased at your local hardware store, online, and at gardening supply stores. Water barrels range from 55 gallons to 75 gallons and cost anywhere from $80 to $200. You can buy them with the spigot or without. The barrels without spigots can be converted using a few tools and parts. You can also negotiate with food manufacturers and large restaurants for their used 55-gallon food grade barrels. Make sure that you clean them well. If the barrel was used for storing oil or any type of chemical, pass on it. It'll be really tough to clean thoroughly and you don't want to gamble with you or your family's safety.

Another method for collecting water for storage is to invest in tub bladders. These cost as low as $20 and are great in case of an emergency. It's as simple as placing the heavy-duty plastic bladder in the tub, connecting it to the spout, and turning on the water. The tub contains the bladder and the bladder fills up within a few minutes. The bladder keeps the water clean and holds up to 100 gallons drinking water. The bladder is even fitted with a siphon pump for when you need to use the water.   You can even get creative with placing these tub bladders in a 55-gallon drum or tub-like homemade structure and running a hose from your tub to the bladder. It's effectively stored in a food grade container and provides clean drinking water at your disposal. It's inexpensive. It would keep your tub clear and it wouldn't require you to move 100 gallons of water. The cost would be the price of the bag, the cost of the container or bladder-holding structure and the normal cost of taking a bath. The water stored in tub bladders will be useable for up to 4 weeks. Utilizing an air compressor, you can flush the pump, nozzle and bladder in a light bleach solution that will keep the bladder cleaner and ready for re-use. Many tub bladders are expected to be single use. So if you find an air compressor on sale, make the investment and save some money.

Some common challenges to water storage are algae, mosquitoes, and clogged spigots. Algae grow as a response to light warming up the water. You can avoid this by adding 1/8 teaspoon to 1/4 teaspoon of unscented regular household bleach per gallon to your water storage. Store the water in a cool, dark place, and keep it covered. Most food grade water barrels are designed to keep out light.

Mosquitoes like to lay eggs in stagnant water. Keeping your water covered is your best defense against mosquitoes and their larvae. Other ways to combat mosquito larvae is to cover the intake with nylon pantyhose. You will need to check the filter often to ensure that the pantyhose don't have any holes at all and isn't deteriorating. The nylon pantyhose is fine enough a filter to keep out mosquitoes seeking to lay eggs but will still allow water to pass through. However, the pantyhose require diligence because the smallest hole will allow mosquitoes.

Another way to combat mosquito larvae is to use Mosquito Dunks. Mosquito Dunks are small ringed products containing the bacteria BTI. It's only toxic to mosquito larvae, lasts 30 days, and treats 100 square feet of water. These rings have an indefinite shelf life so long as they remain dry and unused. You can purchase a 6 pack of Mosquito Dunks for a little as $10. And, Mosquito Dunks can be halved and quartered for use in smaller areas.

The third common problem with water storage is clogged spigots and low water pressure. Here's a simple fix for that. Remove the top of the spigot with a pair of pliers. Water should squirt out due to the pressure release. If this doesn't happen, then use a twig, stick or pipe cleaner to clear the flow path until the water squirts out, clearing the rest of the way. If a clogged filter is also resulting in low pressure, this will rectify that situation. Sometimes low water pressure is caused by low water levels in your storage unit. When you have more water in your water storage unit, you will have better water pressure because the water is creating the pressure. But, the less water you have in your storage unit, the less pressure your will have.

Knowledge of whether water can be made into potable drinking water is important because you don't want to waste your resources on a lost cause. There are ways to filter and purify water for these purposes. A few common ways are boiling, bleach, potable water purification tabs and filters.

Boiling is a great way to remove dangerous bacteria from your water, as is 1/8 teaspoon to 1/4 teaspoon of regular unscented household liquid bleach. In water purification tablets (50 tablets cost about $10), the active ingredient is usually chlorine or iodine and the tablets are another great way to deactivate bacteria, viruses, and parasites. However, water purification tablets do not remove chemicals or sediment from the water nor does it kill Cryptosporidium, which can cause diarrhea. It would be a last step after filtering your water. Filters can be purchased for your water storage or for emergency use in your bug out bag or you can make your own filter.

When you begin making your filter, you will want coffee filters, activated charcoal (2 bottles cost about $10 to $12), rinsed sand, and rinsed gravel (small pebbles or stones). You can use two 5-gallon buckets, or a 2-liter soda bottle for this purpose. Some people even create a larger filtering system using a 5-gallon bucket per ingredient and connecting them through plastic plumbing fittings.

Poke or cut holes in the bottom of the container that will be the actual filter. More small holes as opposed to few large holes are preferable. Insert the coffee filters in the bottom of the container. On top of the coffee filter, place a layer of activated charcoal. Follow that with a layer of sand and another layer of activated charcoal. For your next layer, add another layer of sand and follow that layer with a layer of gravel. Your filter is now complete.

After you pour your water through the filter, check the water for sediment or cloudiness. You may have to pour it through a second time. Next, aerate (put air back into your water) the water by pouring it back and forth from each pitcher or bucket.

The first layer of gravel removes large debris like pebbles, sticks, leaves, bugs, and the like. The sand filters out finer particles too small to be caught by the gravel layer. The layer of activated carbon removes, by absorption, bacteria and some chemicals. This bio-filter can be made quickly and on a smaller scale when you are on the move. Or you can make a larger filter for your water reserve as you use it.

Your family can be involved by calling food manufacturers and large restaurants for 55 gallon food grade barrels. You can have younger children collect pebbles or sand for the filter and rinse them. You family also can help you by building rain catchers or tub bladder units if they are old enough.

When you are prepping on a budget, food and water are very important sections of your emergency pantry but there's more. You'll want to make a list of tools and supplies you will need such as clothing, sanitation supplies, light, fire, or electricity, and tools to help you get the job done and defend your shelter. More on those below...

Clothing

When building an emergency pantry, one very important factor that you need to prep for is different types of weather. You don't want you and your family to find yourselves with a 6-month supply of food and water and no spare clothing. You will want to stock a quality pair of waterproof work boots per member in your party, perhaps an extra pair in a larger size if you still have growing children.

A plethora of cheap, comfortable socks and underwear will keep you and your family with fresh dry undergarments. It might seem like a small thing, but believe me, when you are wet and trying to survive day-to-day, clean, dry undergarments can mean the difference between sanity and losing your mind! If you keep wet clothes and shoes on, you can catch any number of diseases. Of course, the common cold, pneumonia, and the like. One not-so-known problem is trench feet. Trench feet is a condition caused by overexposure to damp, cold, wet, unsanitary conditions, poor circulation, and not allowing your feet to dry. People who have had it in the past are mostly likely to encounter it again. Characteristics of trench feet may be swelling, turning red or blue, or a putrid odor, like decay. More advanced symptoms include open sores, blisters, and fungal infections. If left untreated, gangrene can develop. Wouldn't it be easier to avoid all of that and just pack an extra pair of dry socks? Yes!

As with socks and underwear, you will want to stock shirts and pants. Some opt for quantity over quality, if they have extra room. Some prefer to shell out a bit more money upfront for one or two really well-made items, in hopes they will last longer. The choice is up to you. Cotton-blend is always a good choice. They are comfortable and retain a decent look and feel over multiple periods of wearing. You will also want to invest in some rain gear for you and your family. This time you want to stick with quality over quantity. You don't want a water resistant anything. You want a durable waterproof nylon jacket with treated rip-proof seams and a hood. You want the same quality in rain pants that can be worn over clothing, boots and all for each member in your party, particularly if you're in a climate zone with frequent rainfall.

Make sure to include thermal undershirts and underpants for warmth and shorts and short sleeve t-shirts for hot days. Heat stroke is very common and can be a reoccurring nuisance. Only store clean clothes and label the storage unit or box for each member in your party for some organization. Don't forget to stock up on diapers if you have small children, but wait till they graduate to a new diaper size. This gives you a greater chance of having the right size diaper should disaster strike.

One way that you and your family can save money in this area is utilizing thrift shops on their 1/2 off sale days. At thrift stores, you can find gently used work books, jumpsuits, and more. Learning to repair fabric and materials will be a key factor in making your clothing and materials last. You and your family can even repair your current clothing when it tears and add it to your emergency pantry. You can often find items in thrift stores that people got rid of simply because they didn't want to bother making a few stiches or hems. If you can learn to do some simple repairs, you'll save yourself a ton of money in the long run.

If you are going to repair clothing, you need to stock up on materials to repair with. Sewing kits, zipper repairs, needles, thread, and yarn is a good starting point. For repairing shoes, you'll want to invest in shoe repair kits, heel savers, and sewing awls (for heavy duty fabrics). In the event that the emergency situation isn't resolved within 6 months, investing in yourself by learning to make clothes with a sewing machine, knitting, or crochet is a vital skill that you can barter with.

Now, what about doing laundry? If you do decide on a power generator for your home, you might be tempted with a washer and dryer, and while that method is a faster way to do laundry, it guzzles water, energy, and breaks down clothing faster. Some ways to keep clothing lasting longer is to line dry clothes. Treat stains right away with a stain removing solution. Store only clean clothes and avoid storing clothes in moisture or mildew. Stains and body oils and fluids (like sweat) attract moths and bugs and moisture and mildew break down clothing. Storing clothes with baking soda can help reduce moisture and mildew.

Sanitation and First Aid

Besides starvation and dehydration, sanitation will be one of the leading killers in a disaster. There are some supplies you can acquire that will lessen you and your family's chance of falling victim to disease. First things first: pay attention to scrapes, cuts, bumps, and bruises, and take care of them before they go any further. Isopropyl alcohol and hydrogen peroxide are must have items as an antiseptic. Chances are that any first aid kit will contain antiseptic wipes but, for the long haul, you will want to stock several bottles of each.

If anyone in your party needs special medications or inhalers, you will want to acquire extra beforehand. This can be a difficult task considering the regulations on medication and you may have to speak with your doctor about your options. Other items in this category include hearing aids and extra batteries, or prescription glasses. Most people will overlook having extra of these items in case of emergency; don't be one of those people!

In your first aid kit, whether you buy a prepackaged one or custom make your own, you will want at least a few of these items, if not all of them:

Rolls of gauze with the fasteners: these are useful for sprains, and covering bandaging

Tweezers: Useful for splinters, ticks, and more

Medical scissors (pointed & sharp): Used for removing stitches

Medical scissors (blunt): Used for removing bandages without damaging surrounding skin.

Skin glue: Closing up surface wounds and acts as a liquid Band-Aid

Cotton swabs and cotton balls: Used for cleaning wounds and applying antiseptics, cream, or   ointments

Eye drops: Used for lubricating eyeball

Aspirin is important medicine to stock in your emergency pantry. Aspirin can halt a heart attack because it dilutes the blood and allows for easier passage through the heart. But it doesn't take the place of a doctor so if you can reach a doctor, that would be your best bet. Aspirin also reduces swelling because it's an anti-inflammatory drug in addition to reducing fevers and minor aches and pains.

Of course, for ointments and creams, you want antibiotic ointment to stave off infection and hydrocortisone cream for bug bites, rashes, and run-ins with poison ivy and poison oak. Last but not least, hand sanitizer will come in handy should you have to patch up yourself or others.

For the sake of cleanliness, here are a few items that you and your family should stock and will definitely benefit from:

Cat Litter: I know, I know. You don't have a cat so why in the world would you want to stock cat litter? Well, it's a really useful tool! Soaks like a sponge and it's useful for human waste or biofluids gone awry. It can help reduce mold or moisture from water and soak up any other type of liquid spill.

Bleach: Useful for purifying water and cleaning. Bleach expires and is poisonous in large doses. Use caution in storage & rotation in your pantry and always adhere to directions for usage.

Baking Soda: Use as a toothpaste, deodorizer, cleaning agent and fire extinguisher.

Vinegar: Use as cleaner & deodorizer. Vinegar effectively eliminates cat urine and skunk sprays.

Three 5-Gallon Buckets or Dishpans for cleaning dishes: Use a bucket each to scrape food into, wash dishes, and sanitize dishes.

Body soap, dishwashing soap, sponge, and towels: Soap to clean yourself and your dishes. Use separate towels for dishes and bodies and each member in your party should have their own towel

Facial tissues, toilet paper, washable handkerchiefs, and paper-towels: These help reduce the spread of germs as long as they are properly stored.

Sanitary Napkins: They can also double as a sterile medical pad for a wound.

Electricity, Light, and Fire

You're going to need some electricity and light in a survival situation; that much is a given. How willing are you to rely on your local grid staying online? How comfortable are you without electricity? Some light sources that you'll want to consider are batteries, lamps and oil, and creating your own electricity. Batteries will store for about 2 years in an extremely humid environment but in a dry environment, they will last anywhere from 4 to 6 years. Refrigerated batteries stored in an airtight zip lock bag will last from 6 to 9 years and batteries stored in a freezer will last for 10 years or more. These numbers vary upon the humidity and the temperature, and the quality of battery used. Rechargeable batteries, however, work best at room temperature. Batteries are a prudent investment for emergencies and from the initial emergency till you have time to get situated.

Oil lamps, while they can start fires if dropped, are still a better alternative to candles. With candles, the open flame can start fires with curtains or anything else that gets in its way. The candle can blow out when you need it the most and candles don't actually provide that much light. Oil lamps are brighter than candles and they can be purchased with a light reflector to amplify the light as well. Most oil lamps have a wind guard to protect the flame from going out and they are easier to maneuver due to their sturdy base and handle.

For electricity, your options will be limited to your budget or do-it-yourself skill set. Generators start from $630 for a propane-powered generator or $650 for an oil-powered generator and go way, way higher from there. There are, of course, do-it-yourself resources available for building your own power generators from solar, wind, and water and if you have any handyman skills, these could be a very useful, economical alternative. When considering whether or not to invest in a generator, consider what you will be using it for. You and your family's energy consumption will be significantly reduced in the case of a hunker-down emergency. Nevertheless, electricity may be another component of your preparation that you may want to focus on after your more important and basic supplies are gathered. You might consider low payment layaway plans for purchasing a generator, if you decide that having a steady supply of electricity is essential for your family's plans.

If you plan to make fire, then you need to stock up on items like charcoal, firewood, lighter fluid and tinder. For your lamps, you'll need lamp oil, wicks and the lamps. You can store two lamps to use and have 2 backup or emergency lamps. You may need more lamps for a larger family, of course. Cotton balls soaked in petroleum jelly make for a quick, inexpensive fire starter as well.

While candles are not ideal, some light is better than none at all, so add candles and candle holders to your pantry, as a type of backup to your backup plan. The non-scented candles will attract less attention from bugs and people. As for the fire itself, you will want different ways to create fire, of course. Learn fire-starting techniques if you don't know any already. Teach your spouse, children, and anyone else that will be surviving with you. Stock up on matches, lighters, magnesium and flint starters, waterproof matches and windproof lighters.

Fire can completely change a situation from being cold, wet and unbearable to dry, warm, and manageable. It's important to be smart and safe with your fire, of course. Fires can be seen at night and the smoke can be seen during the day. If you and your family find yourselves in a dangerous situation where your presence is best left unknown, don't advertise your whereabouts via a campfire. If you're bunking in at home and are not in danger from neighbors or predators, a constant fire can be a great mood-booster, not to mention all of its practical uses as well.

General Supplies and Uses

In the area of general supplies, anything that you think you or your family might benefit from can be on this list. I know, that seems a bit too wide open. But really this is your catchall category. These items are not essential to your survival, but they can help. You'll want items such as can openers, reusable plastic dishes, and eating utensils. Toys or books for the kids. Hand-crank radio. Things of that nature.

If you've stocked up seeds for gardening, then it makes sense that you'll want some gardening supplies. A hoe, rake and shovel are a good place to start. And they have multiple uses such as building traps, or using as a weapon against a would-be intruder. A broom and dustpan are also two tools that can help keep your living area cleaner and free of debris. In the event that garbage pick up is suspended, investing in a metal burn barrel is one way idea to eliminate waste.

With you and your family potentially living in an enclosed area, trash is sure to build up and attract bugs, flies, and animals. Include all kinds of bags in your emergency pantry. Garbage bags and grocery bags can be used for trash and freezer bags can be used to help ration food or even keep each family member's personal items separate.

Bug spray, sunscreen, petroleum jelly, lotions, and creams can help protect you from bugs, the sun, and dry skin. Any one of these factors can turn into a rash that can get infected. The idea is to prevent cuts, scrapes, and rashes to prevent infection but some situations cannot be avoided. If that is the case, you will be glad that you will diligent in your medical supplies.

Other items of interest include duct tape, super glue and zip ties. These items are versatile and have multiple functions around the house. Duct tape can aid in sealing up windows and doors. Super glue can help to make repairs to clothes or light items. Zip ties can be used to consolidating equipment or restraining intruders.

Paracord has many uses from hammocks and tents to creating traps for wildlife or a trip wire to alert you of intruders. Paracord can even be intertwined with another rope of paracord to make it stronger and more durable. Many times, the trouble is not with the rope used but with the knot used. Knowing what knot to use and when could save the day. Increase your skill set and knowledge. Pass on the knowledge to your spouse and children. Learn together and grow together.

Lastly, here are a few items that are useful to keep on hand that may be overlooked in your initial planning. Maps of the local area and surrounding larger areas are useful in case you do have to leave your shelter. Writing instruments, pens, pencil, pencil sharpeners, paper, and sharpies can be used to keep young children out of your hair or for writing down your thoughts. Sharpies are always useful for labeling foods, box, and cans. Aluminum foil seems to always have a use, even if it's just cooking by campfire. A spare cell phone that runs on prepaid minutes could be the deciding factor in your situation if you and your family are barricaded in a dangerous zone. If you have any pets, you will want to include extra pet food and extra water for them. Keeping them alive and with you will be an enormous morale booster, so don't forget to plan for Fido. Any comfort foods or sweets that are non-perishable can be included in your pantry. A small treat from time to time can also aid in boosting morale and motivation.

Defense and Security

So, you've built up your pantry and have a whole host of supplies. Excellent. Now comes another problem to address. How do you defend yourself, your family, and your emergency pantry? It is no secret that many people don't really plan for emergency situations beyond a credit card and rushing to the grocery store. Looting and rioting is a real and present danger. The local law enforcement may be so overwhelmed that you are on your own until they arrive. An even scarier situation is that local law enforcement may never arrive. What will you do in that situation?

Some people believe that if they keep to themselves and keep their head down that they will remain unscathed. This is not usually true, as we have seen in the case of a terrorist act (September 11th attacks) or a natural disaster (Hurricane Katrina). People are caught in the crossfire of war and natural disaster everyday. When the aftermath of these events are disorder, people will act as though everyone and everything is fair game. People revert to a more vicious, barbaric state of being when their survival is threatened. Fighting in the grocery stores, fighting in the streets, and people whose goal is to take what you have prepared is a situation that you need to prepare for and it can be deadly for you and your family if you don't.

Some challenges to defense and security are the law and your own code of ethics. The federal law states that defending oneself or others using reasonable force is legal. As a response to an unquestionably unlawful act with reasonable belief that the act will result in fighting with injurious or fatal consequences, defense up to and including deadly force may be used. Some states have a "duty to retreat" clause, with the exceptions that only if the person is unable to safely retreat or they are already in their own home, deadly force may be used. If law enforcement is active when you are presented with a situation or if law and order gets reestablished after your situation is resolved, you may still have to contend with legal fallout. Of course, this will be less important if society has well and truly broken down. In that scenario, it won't matter what the laws and regulations are: you will need to protect your family at all cost.

There are some people who will avoid violence to the extent that it may cost them their life. There are people that believe that negotiating with their attackers can resolve the situation. You have to decide to what extent you are willing to defend yourself, your family, and your preparations. If you perish, will your family be safe? Or will they fall victim to the attackers as well? Most intruders don't stop at "just what they need". If you are willing to do what is necessary to protect and defend you and yours, then you need to prepare your mind and your body. It's not an easy thing to approach, but if you are truly going to be prepared for any situation, it's a vital step along the way.

First things first: raise your awareness. All the guns and self-defense training in the world are useless to you if you are caught unaware. Should you find yourself in a disaster-type situation, you may have to do tasks that require you to pay attention. And it's easy to get so caught up in completing a task that you forget to look around. A way to train yourself to look around is set an alarm every ten minutes. As you do tasks around the house, when your watch or phone goes off, look up and look around. Eventually, as you're working, you'll find yourself looking periodically and you will notice when time has passed and you haven't looked around. You'll become more aware of your surroundings. You'll notice when something doesn't seem quite right. This can be the difference between survival or not one day, so take the time to practice these skills now.

One way to involve your family, if they are old enough, is to have them take turns as watchers. Teach them what to be aware of such as sounds of movement, moving bushes, concealed people, people who are trying to conceal themselves, suspicious behavior or activity, and groups of people. No matter how trivial, train yourself and your family to watch with their eyes and their ears. At the end of the task or activity, ask what they have seen and why it caught their attention.

Some ways to prepare for to defend yourself and you family is increasing your knowledge in both unarmed self-defense and armed self-defense. You will want to explore non-lethal and lethal methods of defense. Above all, the mindset to take action is important. Know what danger looks like and take action.

Next, look at your defense options. You can increase your knowledge by taking self-defense classes. A few well-learned basic moves trump a bunch of over-elegant half-learned moves. And, anything can be a defense weapon in a survival situation, like a golf club, sturdy walking stick, baseball bat, rock, cane, flashlight, or even a pen.

Non-lethal defense weapons can be weapons such as these:

Batons ($16 online): Batons can give you the advantage of reach.

Stun Guns ($11 online): It temporarily disables your assailant in close encounters due to an electrical shock.

Expandable Stun Baton ($40 online): Gives you the advantage of reach plus the whole baton (minus the handle) stuns. If your assailant tries to grab the baton, they get stunned.

Pepper Spray ($16 online): It temporarily disables your assailant with blinding liquid, pain causing pepper spray.

Pepper Gun ($55 online): Trigger-activated and shoots accurate and continuous stream of   pepper spray up to 25 ft.

Any one of these weapons can be kept in your home for close encounters. For lethal weapons, you might consider investing in a gun. There are several types of guns and if you are considering a gun as a measure of defense or otherwise, there are a few things you need to know. The most common types of guns owned by civilians are pistols, revolvers, shotguns, and rifles.

Pistols are loaded with clips and the clips are loaded with bullets. Revolvers differ from pistols in that the bullets are slid directly into the individual bullet chambers and not slid into a clip, which is then inserted into a gun. An advantage of pistols is that clips hold more bullets than a revolver and you can carry spare clips. An advantage of revolvers is that you don't need a clip to load the gun. You can carry the spare ammo on your person and reload as need. Pistols and revolvers are accurate in long distances (up to a certain range) or close encounters.

A shotgun is smoothbore, meaning that the inside of the barrel has no grooves and is either single-barreled or double-barreled. A single-barrel dispenses one shotgun shell; a double barrel dispenses two shotgun shells, one from each barrel. Shotguns are more accurate in close encounters and not very accurate in long range. They do a considerable amount more damage than a standard pistol or revolver, however.

Rifles have a barrel 16 inches or longer and the inside of the barrel has spiraled, parallel grooves (hence the term, rifle) that spin the bullet as it moves out the barrel upon discharge. This allows for a longer range of accuracy. Rifles can be used for hunting or by a watcher, as can a shotgun. A pistol or revolver can be carried on your person and concealed so as not to draw attention.

Owning a gun in your home can give you and your family a real sense of security. It is a deterrent to would-be intruders and can induce instant compliance. Rifles can be used to hunt wildlife and provide dinner should your disaster situation last longer than your emergency pantry. Guns can be the factor that increases your advantage in a confrontation.

The other side of the coin is that a gun in the home increases the risks of accidents. Even when the gun is securely locked, the possibility that your children will gain access somehow is present. Guns at home are frequently used in suicides and accidental shootings of a family members, neighbors, and friends. Even when you take every precaution imaginable, the unimaginable can happen. This is something you need to discuss with your family and take the proper steps, such as gun safety training, hunting lessons, and proper gun ownership courses.

Other challenges to gun ownership are presented by the law. The federal law prohibits certain people from owning guns such as people with felonies, misdemeanors, or dishonorable discharge from the military. Fugitives, illegal aliens, people diagnosed with mental illness, people who have renounced their U.S. Citizenship, people convicted of a domestic violence misdemeanor, and people subject to particular restraining orders are also on the list prohibiting gun ownership. States may require registration, licenses or permits to own, open carry, conceal carry, or transport. Most all states require background checks for firearm purchases. Some states recognize others states laws and some do not. If you decide that having a gun present is necessary for you and your family, do research on what options meets your and your family's needs. From there, create a safety plan with your family to help lower the risk of a gun-related accident.

You can never plan for every scenario that could happen or go wrong. Should you find yourselves in a survival situation, there are some safety precautions you and your family can take. If you have to go anywhere, don't go ill prepared and never go alone. Have a weapon to defend yourself and someone by your side to double your chances of success. If your family consists of two adults and small children, your decisions are more delicate. Perhaps you can have checkpoints and the other adult can act as a watcher, scanning the area for what you cannot see. At night, don't use any light, candles, or fire. A single candle can be distinguished up to 30 miles away by the human eye. If light is absolutely necessary, keep your curtains closed and your windows boarded up.

By having the knowledge and mindset to defend yourself and your family at any cost, you will have increased your chances of survival but there is one more *very* important concept to understand. That is that you should always try to avoid avoidable situations. You may be armed to the teeth to defend and protect, but each encounter slurps up resources and presents a possibility of injury and infection. If you can achieve your goal without a confrontation, do it. Make the smarter choice and increase your chances of long-term survival.

Securing Your Shelter

Another step in preparing yourself and your family is fortifying your home, also known as your Shelter-In-Place. Outside your home you will want objects that alert you to an outsider's presence. One way to achieve this is to have floodlights or motion sensor strobe lights outside your home. Another way to alert you and your family is to have watchers or a guard dog. Or, you can collect cans, put a few marbles or noisemakers inside and string them low to the ground. You can even have rope pulled taut on the ground tied to the cans in the trees, so when the rope is stepped on, the cans in the trees make noise. If you need to, you can even create pit traps. None of these need to cost much money.

Any easy trap is to dig a deep hole at least 12 feet deep. Cover the hole with a light grid of twigs that will easily snap under pressure. Then, cover the grid with leaves. Of course, you don't want your family or the mailman wandering through that area. It may be better to dig the hole after the disaster strikes.

From inside the house, what you need to focus on securing are the entrances, exits, windows, and vents. While some people go all the way with bars on the windows, some people don't like the idea of getting trapped in their own homes should an intruder get the best of them. A compromise is to have a way to quickly fortify your home at a moment's notice.

For boarding up your windows and doors, you'll want to have enough wood to block all your windows and doors. Cut the wood to fit your windows and doors. Invest in an electric drill (as low as $25); keep it fully charged and next to your pre-cut wood. Screws are favored over nails in this case, should you have to remove the panels and make a getaway. When you install the wood panels, do it on the inside of the house and behind the curtains. There's no need to advertise your presence. Store the wood in the room. Make sure that it's easily accessible.

In case of a biological airborne attack, you'll want to secure every door, window, vent, crack and crevice that could let air from the outside flow inside. To do this, get plastic sheeting ($5 per 10 ft. x 10 ft. online). You'll want plastic thicker than plastic food wrap. Pre-cut the sheeting to fit all your windows and doors in each room because you never know what room you will be in. Pre-cut sheeting for every vent and outlet, and don't forget the vent over your stove. The official rule for breathable air is 10ft x 10ft of space per person to prevent carbon dioxide build up. This is for up to 5 hours. To secure your room, securely duct tape the sheeting over the windows, doors, vents, and outlets and duct tape any cracks. The goal is to prevent any outside air from entering the room. To store your supplies, have a storage unit marked (Shelter-in-place sheeting) and easily accessible. Store your pre-cut plastic sheeting and a couple rolls of duct tape in each room.

Insides defenses could include keeping a club, walking stick, baseball bat, knife or any object that can be used for defense in each room in an easily accessible spot that does not change. A note of interest is operational security. You don't want your preparations and defenses to be public knowledge. Your nice neighbors may have a nastier side in a disaster scenario. Communicating to your family the importance of silence is imperative for the sake of survival. Also, suppose stragglers wander by, posing no threat, seeking a meal and some water. Will you deny them? Will you feed them? There's no way to know if they won't return with a mob to take your food. You have to decide what you can spare, if anything at all. If your emergency pantry is strict in rations, then you have nothing to spare. Not sticking to your preparedness plan is like not having a plan at all.

Plan B

Plan B is to Bug Out. Bugging out means leaving your home or shelter and heading to another home or shelter. This bug out location should be safe, secure, and stocked with a few days worth of food for you and your family until you can get situated. This might be a cousin's house on a farm, your parents' house if they have a basement, or a friend in your prepper network. If you have been building an emergency pantry at your home, the idea of leaving your preparations behind might not be resonating with you at all.

There are a few reasons that might lead you to move into Plan B. If your emergency food pantry has depleted, it's time act. You might think to check abandoned houses or start hunting for food. But what if the houses have already been sacked, are still occupied, and the animals are gone? Other reasons that would lead to bugging out are hostility and environmental danger. Even with the best fortified shelters, it only takes time and consistency to eventually become overwhelmed by attackers. And a top of the line, fortified shelter isn't going to stop a flood, wildfire, hurricane, or another natural disaster. It might withstand one, but only for so long. Obviously, bugging out is not going to be your first action, but if it's going to an action at all, it needs to be planned.

Decide on where your bug out location is going to be. If it's a friend or family member's property, you may want to keep them informed of your possible arrival pending a catastrophe. You and your family might be at different locations when disaster strikes and if none of you can make it to your shelter-in-place due to hazard and road conditions, how do you reconnect? Can your important documents be recovered? Who is going to pick up the kids from school? Before you ever reach that scenario, you need to have predetermined checkpoints and a plan of action in place. Everyone in the family should know their checkpoint and know where they are headed if disaster strikes. You could perhaps station one checkpoint for each side of your town or city. Or you could have different checkpoints for different days of the week. Such as, Mondays and Wednesdays and Fridays are checkpoint 1 and Saturdays, Sundays, Tuesdays, and Thursdays are checkpoint 2.

Now, bugging out is only as good as your route. If your normal exit route takes you and your family back into the fray, then your escape route is compromised. One way to avoid a compromised escape route is to have Alternate Escape Routes.

Alternate escape routes are routes that are basically another way to get where you're going. It helps if they are less commonly used, traffic-jam free and lead out towards your destination. Many times when cities are evacuated, the main roads and normal routes are cluttered with cars and people. Your alternate escape routes will allow you to exit the city and avoid being stuck out in the open, in a crowd of scared, angry citizens, with your family.

If you can, recover your safe box with all your important documents in it. These include birth certificates, driver' licenses, marriage license, gun permits or registrations (if you have one), social security cards and anything else that is important. You may even want to include a few photos for a taste of home.

Involving Your Family

Family can be a hard thing to motivate when it comes to prepping. Transitioning to a lifestyle of preparedness means getting vigilant and prudent and *staying* vigilant and prudent. The change is not always welcome. Some ways to involve your family is to communicate that "the phase" will not pass. Talk with them about the benefits of a preparedness lifestyle. Explore techniques and put them to the test, such as a your gear, skills, and awareness. Make sure they know how to use waterproof matches or magnesium and flint and how to safely build a fire. As you learn, teach them also. Teach them different knots and paracord uses and how to build traps and tarp lean-tos, and how to hunt and garden. Camping is as good a time as any to test your skills. Make it a fun family event to go camping once a month or so. This will help everyone in your family become used to the outdoor, survival lifestyle. After all, you want to know what techniques and gear work well and which ones don't. Waiting until disaster strikes to find out what works is an ill-advised plan.

If you have made a list for the items in your emergency pantry, perhaps let your family loose in the thrift store or flea market. Set them on a hunt for the lowest priced pantry items. One way to really get your family involved is by having them build their own bug out bags. It can be a really fun exercise for children, and it helps them feel invested and responsible for something.

Having your family involved in the evacuation plans, alternate escape routes and checkpoints is another way to have them involved. The more invested they are in the plan from the beginning, the more likely they are to remember the plan because they were a part of building it rather than merely being told what the plan is.

Your family can also be involved in the maintenance of your emergency pantry. As you acquire supplies and food on your list, you will want to check it off the list. You can have someone label the food with the date acquired, the expiration date and the ingredients the day it's brought home. Next, create a separate inventory list of what you have acquired so far. A subject notebook will do. In this notebook will be a Column 1 with the name of the food or supplies. Column 2 will have the date acquired. Column 3 will have the Expiration date.

Write down your entire emergency pantry as you acquire it. This is also a task that a family member can do. For rotation, you can have a family member check the dates in the inventory book weekly and pull all foods or supplies that expire in 1 or 2 months time. You can use these items by rotating them out. As you repurchase these items, rotate them back into your budget and emergency pantry. Label the items and record them in your inventory book. This ensures that your pantry is up-to-date with useable goods and your family isn't wasting any food or money by letting items go bad.

Labeling cans and writing an inventory can get tedious, so mix things up by rotating weekly shifts. These shifts will add responsibility and keep the preparedness lifestyle at the forefront of your family's mind. Continue to stress that scared people are angry people and can become dangerous people. The need for concealing your plans and preparations is imperative as is avoiding avoidable situations.

Prepping on a budget has its challenges, but you and your family can't afford to *not* prepare. Prepping may seem like a lot of work for a never-ending job. Don't let yourself get discouraged before you ever begin. Any preparation, no matter how small is one more advantage you and your family will have. Even when you are ever so slowly moving forward, it is better than standing still, and you and your family will benefit from it. Go steady but go forward.

Closing Thoughts

Once you have prepared for natural disasters and assessed how well your home is protected, then it's time to make sure that you and your family are ready to get where you need to be. Prepping is a lifestyle and a choice that you can make today. It can seem intimidating at first, but the sooner you start, the better off you will be. It doesn't have to break the bank and, if done correctly, it will even help you save a lot of money in the long run. From buying food in bulk, to using coupons, to starting early and saving often, there are many ways to make prepping more affordable and more achievable for any person or family.

You don't need to spend money on every latest gadget and toy, every item marketed as a "must-have" or a "life-saver". There are now entire businesses set up just to try to convince people that they *need* to buy a certain item to survive, or they *just must* subscribe to a monthly service and receive a new survival item every month.

Simply not true! People have been prepping for generations without any of those things, and those same prepping principles are still more than useful today.

At its core, prepping is about securing the future of you and your family. So it makes sense that a big part of this equation is to do it all without incurring huge amounts of debts and making yourself beholden to some big bank or credit card company. We need to be prepared not only physically, but mentally and financially as well. We have no way of knowing what events will be coming our way, but it only makes sense to prepare the same, whether it's a natural disaster, a society disaster, or a global financial collapse. If you follow the principles of prepping on a budget, you'll be in the best possible position to deal with whatever comes our way. And really, that's what this is all about!

*****

If you've enjoyed this book, **please** consider leaving a review and letting others know what you thought!

Sign up for Robert's Mailing List to be notified of **New Releases** and **Special Sales**: http://eepurl.com/zvm11

No Spam – he promises!

*****

Other Books by Robert Paine:
Prepper's Pantry: A Survival Food Guide

www.ingramcontent.com/pod-product-compliance
Lightning Source LLC
Chambersburg PA
CBHW060225290526
45789CB00003B/1411